S·H·P

what is
history ?

Y7

a *starter* unit for key stage 3

Ian Dawson

JOHN MURRAY

The Schools History Project

The Project was set up in 1972, with the aim of improving the study of history for students aged 13–16. This involved a reconsideration of the ways in which history contributes to the educational needs of young people. The Project devised new objectives, new criteria for planning and developing courses, and the materials to support them. New examinations, requiring new methods of assessment, also had to be developed. These have continued to be popular. The advent of GCSE in 1987 led to the expansion of Project approaches into other syllabuses.

The Schools History Project has been based at Trinity and All Saints College, Leeds, since 1978, from where it supports teachers through a biennial Bulletin, regular INSET, an annual Conference and a website (www.tasc.ac.uk/shp).

Since the National Curriculum was drawn up in 1991, the Project has continued to expand its publications, bringing its ideas to courses for Key Stage 3 as well as a range of GCSE and A level specifications.

Acknowledgements

Cover British Museum, London, UK/Bridgeman Art Library; **p.i** British Museum, London, UK/Bridgeman Art Library; **p.2** *t* York Archaeological Trust, *bl* Syon House, Middlesex, UK/Bridgeman Art Library, *br* © Richard Olivier/Corbis; **p.3** Topham Picturepoint; **p.6** *fig.1* The Art Archive/Dagli Orti, *fig.2* The Art Archive/*The Beano* © D.C. Thomson & Co. Ltd, *fig.3* The Art Archive, *fig.4* The Art Archive/Bibliothèque des Arts Décoratifs, Paris/Dagli Orti, *fig.5* The Art Archive/Magdalene College, Cambridge/Eileen Tweedy, *fig.6* © Vince Streano/Corbis; **p.7** *fig.7* Mary Evans Picture Library, *fig.8* Louvre, Paris, France/Bridgeman Art Library, *fig.9* Louvre, Paris, France/Peter Willi/Bridgeman Art Library, *fig.10* The Art Archive/British Library, *fig.11* The Art Archive/Museo della Civilita Romana, Rome/Dagli Orti, *fig.12* Copyright Reading Museum Service (Reading Borough Council). All rights reserved., *fig.13* British Museum, London, UK/Bridgeman Art Library, *fig.14* Private Collection/The Stapleton Collection/Bridgeman Art Library, *fig.15* The Art Archive/Museo della Sibaritide, Sibari/Dagli Orti, *fig.16* © University Museum of Cultural Heritage – University of Oslo, Norway (photo: Eirik Irgens Johnsen), *fig.17* Lambeth Palace Library, London, UK/Bridgeman Art Library, *fig.18* Cheltenham Art Gallery and Museums, Gloucestershire, UK/Bridgeman Art Library; **p.8** *t* English Heritage, *c* Fotomas Index, *b* Private Collection/Christies Images/Bridgeman Art Library; **p.9** *t* The Art Archive/Public Record Office, London, *b* Guildhall Art Library, Corporation of London, UK/Bridgeman Art Library; **p.12** *both* York Archaeological Trust; **p.14** © Museum of London; **p.16** *t* British Museum, London, UK/Bridgeman Art Library, *b* The British Library; **p.23** *l* Cover illustration © Martin Brown 1994. All rights reserved. Reproduced by kind permission of Scholastic Ltd, *cl Pride and Prejudice* DVD © BBC Worldwide, *cr* Crown Copyright Historic Royal Palaces (photo: Paddy Eckersley); **p.28** © Michael Nicholson/Corbis; **p.29** The Art Archive/Musée du Château de Versailles/Dagli Orti; **p.31** © Richard Olivier/Corbis; **p.32** Camera Press; **p.33** *t* Topham Picturepoint, *b* popperfoto.com; **p.35** photograph by Hanlon, London/© Val Wilmer Archive; **p.41** Private Collection/Bridgeman Art Library.

(t = top, b = bottom, l = left, r = right, c = centre)

While every effort has been made to contact copyright holders, the Publishers apologise for any omissions, which they will be pleased to rectify at the earliest opportunity.

© Ian Dawson 2003
First published in 2003 by
John Murray (Publishers) Ltd, a member of the Hodder Headline Group
338 Euston Road
London NW1 3BH

Layouts by Amanda Hawkes
Artwork by Art Construction, Peter Bull, Jon Davis (Linden Artists), Conny Jude, Tony Randell, Steve Smith
Cover design by John Townson/Creation
Typeset in 12/14 pt Meridien Roman by Fakenham Photosetting Ltd, Fakenham, Norfolk
Printed and bound in Spain by Bookprint, S.L., Barcelona

A catalogue entry for this book is available from the British Library

Pupil's Book ISBN 0 7195 7961 9
Teacher's Resource Book ISBN 0 7195 7962 7

What is History?

1 You probably already know a lot about History.
<u>How</u> would you complete this sentence: 'History is . . .'?
Here are some of our ideas:

History is . . .

. . . finding out about **the past.**

. . . finding out about **real people** doing brave things, ordinary things, amazing things, terrible **things**.

. . . using **sources**.

. . . asking **questions** and sorting out **answers**.

. . . ???

Contents

This book gives you our ideas of what History is all about – and how you can get better at it.

There are seven zones for you to investigate:

- start with the Time Zone
- finish with the Improvement Zone
- but, in between, you can tackle the other five zones in whatever order you like.

Good luck!

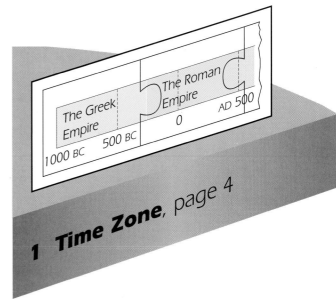

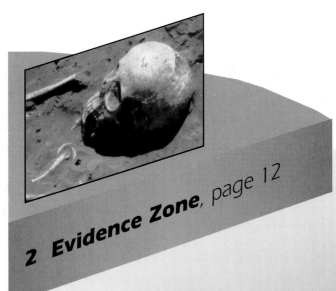

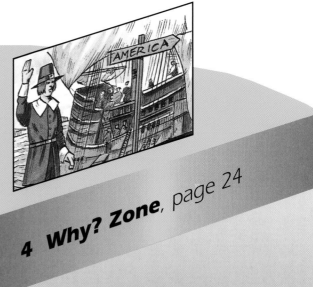

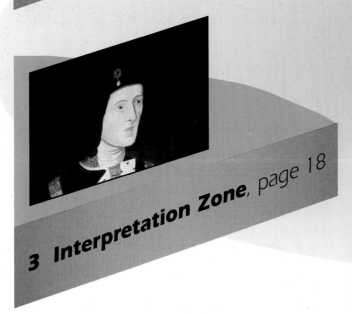

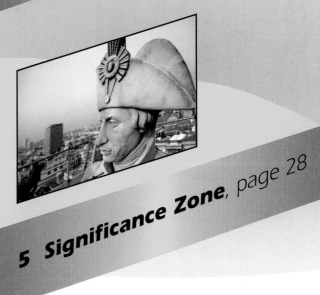

In every zone you will find:

1 Activities to do

Think
? <u>Discussion</u> questions to improve your thinking skills

■ **History words**
Like any subject History has its own vocabulary. Important History words are SHOWN LIKE THIS. You should find out what they mean and use them to make your own glossary. If you use these words properly you will find History much easier (and you might impress your teacher!)

Big ideas
Highlights the main ideas and skills you need to do History

Now turn over to the Time Zone.

What belongs when?

Time Zone

■ Level One

The Time Zone is made up of three levels. In each level you will be shown people, buildings or objects from the past. Your task is to piece them together so they are in the right CHRONOLOGICAL ORDER, a bit like putting a jigsaw together. When you have finished all three levels, you'll be able to see all of history spread out in front of you!

Level One may be quite easy because you will recognise the people and buildings from the history you have already studied.

> ■ **History words**
> Chronological order means date order. When things are in chronological order the earliest comes first.

1 Can you match up the people below with the buildings from the same PERIOD of history on page 5? There's one person for each building.

Now you've paired up the people and the buildings:

(2) Which of these period labels goes with each pair?

The Anglo-Saxons and Vikings

The ANCIENT Greeks

The Romans

The Tudors

The Twentieth Century

The Victorians

(3) List the six periods in chronological order – putting the oldest first.

Think

? <u>How</u> did you decide which people and buildings belonged together? For example, what clues did you use in the pictures?

? <u>How</u> did you decide what order the periods go in? For example, did you start with one you knew and then work around that one?

■ Level Two

This level works just like the last one – but there's more of it!

1. Here's a real jumble of things from the past. Your task is to match them up with the people from the six historical periods you can see below.

2. If you have been given sorting cards by your teacher:
   a) group them together into periods
   b) paste each group of period cards onto separate sheets.

The Ancient Greeks

The Romans

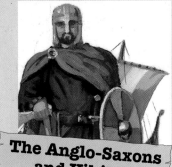

The Anglo-Saxons and Vikings

The Tudors

The Victorians

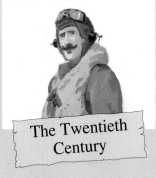

The Twentieth Century

8

11

12

10

APPIVS CLAVDIVS
C·F·CAECVS
CENSOR·COS·BIS·DICT·INTERREX·III
TR·II·AED·CVR·II·Q· ... ·SOL
PLVR·A·OPPIDA·DESAM...
SABINORVM·ET·TVS...
TVM·FVDIT·PACEM...
REGE·PROHIBVIT·IN...
APPIAM·SIRAVIF...
VRBEM·ADDVXIT·A...
FECIT...

13

14

THE
LIFE AND ADVENTURES
OF
NICHOLAS
NICKLEBY

15

16

17 he most wonderfull
and true storie, of a certaine Witch
named Alse Gooderige of Stapen hill,
who was arraigned and conuicted at Darbie
at the Assises there.

As also a true report of the strange torments of Thomas
Darling, a boy of thirteene yeres of age, that was pos-
sessed by the Deuill, with his horrible fittes and terrible Apparitions by him vttered at Burton vpon
Trent in the Countie of Stafford, and of his maruel-
lous deliuerance.

Printed at London for I.O. 1597.
BIBLIOTHECA

18

Think
? <u>Which</u> period was
the easiest to sort?
? <u>Why</u> do you think it
was the easiest?

■ Level Three

Now for the last level of the Time Zone. Here are all the periods of history that you have been sorting out, but look! There are two gaps. These are new periods.

1. Work out which of the people and other objects on these pages go in which gap.

2. What do you think the two periods might be called?

1

2

3

4

?
_____

The Anglo-Saxons and Vikings

The Romans

The Ancient Greeks

The Twentieth Century and after

Industrial and Victorian Britain

?

The Tudors

5

6

7

8

Think
? Which of the periods of history that you have studied is <u>your favourite</u>?
? <u>Why</u> is it your favourite?

time zone time zone time zone time zone time zone time zone time

9

Time Zone

The Big Ideas

In this zone you practised two skills:

■ **sorting** people, objects and events into periods
■ **sequencing** periods.

History is . . .

chronology: putting people, periods and events in the right order!

Know your periods . . .

We divide the past up into chunks that we call 'periods of history'. They are usually named after people or events.

The Stuarts

The Tudors

Medieval

(1) Do you know why the Tudor period is called the Tudor period?

(2) 'MEDIEVAL' means 'Middle Ages'. What was it the middle of?

Period names are 'shorthand'. They save time. When someone says 'The Tudors' to you, you know what they mean without them having to go into long explanations such as, 'You know, the time when Henry VIII lived – and he had all those wives; and lived in big palaces; and argued with the Pope . . . You know!'

... watch out for anachronisms

An ANACHRONISM is something that is out of place. It is in the wrong place or period. The more you find out about history the better you will become at spotting anachronisms.

(3) Can you spot some anachronisms in this picture?

I wish I'd been a Tudor king.

... and make connections

Every person or event in history fits into a period (like files fit into folders). As you file away each new discovery about a period it helps you connect it to what you already know about that period.

And here is another really big idea about History!

History is ...

enquiry. HISTORICAL ENQUIRY means asking and answering questions about history. All the 'stuff' you sorted on pages 4–9 means little until you are using it to answer some questions. The reason people study history in the first place is because they have questions about the past that they want answers to.

WHAT NEXT?
Which zone are you going to INVESTIGATE next? In this book you can choose! Turn to pages 2–3 to see the choices.

(4) Choose one period from pages 8–9. What questions would you like to ask about it? You might use these starters for your questions: How? Who? What? Where? Why? When?

2 *Evidence Zone*

The Skeletons in the Fields

Clue A

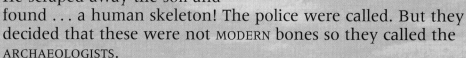

1 What questions do you have about these bones? Write them down.

In 1956 this skull was found on the banks of the River Ouse, near the village of Riccall in Yorkshire. A farmer digging his crops felt his spade hit something hard. He scraped away the soil and found ... a human skeleton! The police were called. But they decided that these were not MODERN bones so they called the ARCHAEOLOGISTS.

The archaeologists dug trenches to see what else they could find. They found 46 more human skeletons. They could not identify the sex of all the skeletons but there were at least 28 men, 2 women and 5 children aged 5–12. They checked back in local history books and discovered that other bones had been found at the same spot in the 1830s and that ten more human skulls had been found in 1880. Much later on, in the 1980s, they found a further 23 skeletons.

So the enquiry became: Who were these people, and how did they die? That will be your enquiry too. And you will use the same clues as the archaeologists. What will you make of these clues?

■ **Who were these people and how did they die?**

(2) Here are the next two clues to help you with this enquiry. Do they give
you any ideas about who the people in Clue A were and how they might have died?

Clue B
Riccall was near the site of two famous battles that were fought in 1066.

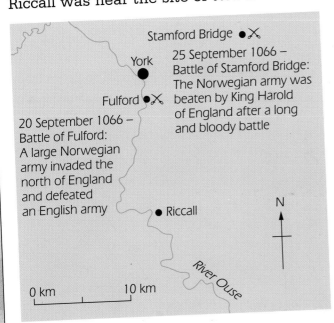

Stamford Bridge ●✗

York ●

25 September 1066 –
Battle of Stamford Bridge:
The Norwegian army was
beaten by King Harold
of England after a long
and bloody battle

Fulford ●✗

20 September 1066 –
Battle of Fulford:
A large Norwegian
army invaded the
north of England
and defeated
an English army

● Riccall

River Ouse

0 km ___ 10 km

N

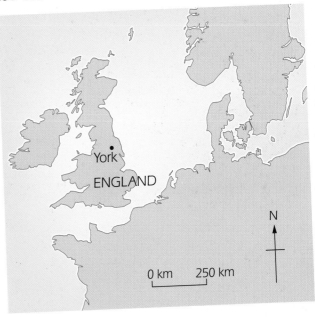

York ●

ENGLAND

0 km ___ 250 km

N

Clue C
Historians
checked
whether there
had ever been
a church near
the field where
the bones had
been found.
There had not.

(3) From the EVIDENCE in Clues A–C you probably already have a possible idea of
who these people were and how they died. Historians call a possible
answer a HYPOTHESIS. Before you turn the page write down your hypothesis.

Use Clues D–H to test your hypothesis.

(1) Start with the clue you think will be most useful. Does it support your hypothesis or does it suggest another answer?

(2) Now look carefully at the rest of the clues in turn.

Clue D

Scientists examined the bones of the skeletons very carefully. On many of the bones they found cut marks like this that looked as if they had been made by swords or axes

One skeleton had a deep cut that must have been the result of a stab wound through the stomach

Clue E

The probable route of the Norwegian soldiers as they tried to get back to their ships after the Battle of Stamford Bridge

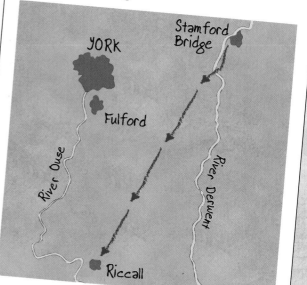

Clue F

Saxon and Viking weapons. These were the kinds of weapons used at the Battles of Fulford and Stamford Bridge.

How the weapons were used

Clue G

An extract from the Anglo-Saxon Chronicle for 1066. This was a record of the main events of each year written by English monks. This account of the Battle of Stamford Bridge had been written by the 1080s.

King Harald of Norway sailed up the River Ouse towards York with 300 ships. King Harold of England was in the south but went northwards day and night as quickly as he could.

5 Before Harold could get there, Earl Edwin and Earl Morcar fought the invading Norwegians but many of their army fled or were killed. The Norwegians won the battle.

Then King Harold of England and a large force of English soldiers took the Norwegians by surprise at Stamford Bridge. They fought strenuously until late in the day. One of the

10 Norwegians stood on the narrow bridge and held off the English army so that they could not cross the bridge or win victory. An Englishman shot an arrow but missed. Then another Englishman crept under the bridge and stabbed the Norwegian from beneath.

15 Then Harold and his army went over the bridge and killed King Harald Hardrada and large numbers of Norwegians. The surviving Norwegians fled. The English pursued them and attacked them fiercely until they reached their ships. Some were drowned and some burned and some killed in

20 various ways so that few survived. The King let the survivors go home in 24 ships.

Who's Who

King of England – Harold. He had been king for just 9 months.

King of Norway – Harald Hardrada. He wanted to conquer England and become king himself.

Clue H

Scientists examined the teeth from six of the skeletons. Scientists can tell which region people grew up in from their teeth. This is because traces of the water that children drink stay in their teeth for ever. The tests on the teeth of the skeletons showed that the people grew up in the blue areas on the map.

Think

? Which clue did you expect to be most useful to check your hypothesis?

? Why did you pick that one?

? Did it turn out to be the most useful one in the end?

Evidence Zone

The Big Ideas

▼ **SOURCE A** A helmet found by archaeologists on a dig at Sutton Hoo in East Anglia. The helmet is from the 600s – the Anglo-Saxon period.

History is . . .

using SOURCES. Sources are things left from the past. They are the clues that tell us about the past, for example about how people used to live, what they did and what they thought.

All sorts of things are sources – DOCUMENTS (written sources), pictures, buildings, ARTEFACTS (that's the word for objects from the past such as spoons or pottery bowls or clothing) and even skeletons!

In this zone you practised one main skill – using sources to pursue an enquiry.

1 What kinds of sources are Sources A and B?

2 What can you learn from each of the sources about Anglo-Saxon life?

Think

? Imagine historians in 200 years' time investigating life today. What <u>kinds</u> of sources would you recommend they use to find out about your life?

? <u>Why</u> will it be easier to find out about life in the early 21st century than life in the year 1000 (the time of the Anglo-Saxons)?

▼ **SOURCE B** A section from the Anglo-Saxon Chronicle. This is what the actual source in Clue G on page 15 looks like.

evidence zone ■ evidence zone ■ evidence zone ■ evidence zone ■ evidence zone ■ evidence zone ■ evide

History is . . .

using sources . . . carefully. One of the skills in using sources is deciding whether to trust what they say!

(3) Why might a document like Clue G (on page 15) NOT be trusted to tell the truth?

(4) What questions would you ask about a source before deciding whether it can be trusted? Make a list. Compare it with our checklist which you can get from your teacher.

History is . . .

sometimes uncertain. We can't always find **definite** answers in History because we don't have enough sources. Therefore, when you work out an answer to a question such as 'Who were they and how did they die?', you need to say how definite your answer is.

(5) Which of the options in the drawing below would best fit your answer to the enquiry about The Skeletons in the Field?

Think
? Would you have been more sure or less sure if you did <u>not</u> have Clue H (page 15)?

I have a definite answer to this enquiry. I am **completely certain** about my answer.

My answer is **probably right** but I really need a little more evidence to be completely certain.

I have a **possible answer** to this enquiry but I really need a lot more evidence to be certain.

I am **very unsure**. I do not have enough evidence to suggest any answer to the enquiry.

WHAT NEXT?
Which zone are you going to investigate next? Turn to pages 2-3 to see the choices.

3 Was King Richard III an evil murderer?

Interpretation Zone

An INTERPRETATION of history is simply someone's version of history. Look at the story of King Richard III on these two pages. It contains facts but these facts have been presented in a certain way. The writer has interpreted the facts to present Richard as … as what? That is for you to work out.

In this Interpretation Zone you will **test** this interpretation of Richard and then try to **explain** how this interpretation arose.

1 Work in pairs. Read the story strip about Richard III. What impression does the story give you of Richard? Choose from these words:

caring	failure	ruthless	clever
cruel	heroic	brave	scheming

2 Who do you think might have created this interpretation of Richard III? (There's a clue in the story.)

Fact and opinion
This interpretation of Richard's story includes facts but it also includes opinions. Can you tell the difference?

3 Which of the following are facts? Which are opinions?

a) Richard III was crowned King of England in 1483.
b) Richard III was an evil man who murdered his nephews.
c) Richard III was a successful king.
d) Richard III was killed at the Battle of Bosworth in 1485.

Think
? How can you tell that this writer does not like Richard? What words or phrases give it away?

RICHARD III — THE KING WHO MURDERED HIS NEPHEWS

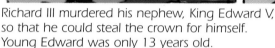

Richard III murdered his nephew, King Edward V, so that he could steal the crown for himself. Young Edward was only 13 years old.

This boy's father and mother were not legally married so he cannot be king!

Richard now had the young king in his power. He invented a story that the boy was illegitimate and so could not be king.

This brutal slaughter of innocent children shocked people all over Europe. Many men bravely risked their lives to fight against Richard.

Richard had always been selfish and ruthless. While his brother was king, Richard used all kinds of tricks and plots to build up his own riches and power. He even used the royal army to take over land for himself in Scotland.

In 1483 King Edward IV suddenly died. His young son became Edward V. Richard tricked the young king and his advisers by pretending to be friendly.

But soon Richard threw the advisers into prison. Then he had them executed without trial.

Richard savagely executed anyone who opposed him and had himself crowned King Richard III.

Next came the worst part of the story. Richard had young Edward and his brother cruelly murdered in the Tower of London. They are still known as the 'Princes in the Tower'.

We want Henry as our king!

Richard crushed the rebellion. The survivors escaped Richard's revenge and fled to France to join Henry Tudor, a brave and noble man – so different from Richard.

Henry Tudor invaded England in August 1485. At last England might get rid of the tyrant Richard.

Richard was killed at the Battle of Bosworth. Henry became King Henry VII, the first of the great Tudor monarchs.

■ Did Richard kill the Princes in the Tower? Be a detective!

An interpretation first needs to be **tested**. This means checking it against the facts and against other evidence. It would take a long time to test the whole of the story strip so we'll focus on just one issue: Did Richard III really murder his nephews?

1 Here is your detective sheet. Use the clues on these two pages to fill out as much as you can.

Detective report	
Question	**Your answer (✓, X, or ?) and which source shows this. Add comments if you need to.**
Was there definitely a murder? For example, were the princes' **bodies** ever found?	
Did Richard have an **opportunity** to have the princes killed?	
Is there any **incriminating evidence** – such as a murder weapon – **proving** that Richard was the murderer?	
Is there any **evidence** that suggests that Richard could be the murderer?	
Is there any **evidence** that suggests that Richard might be innocent?	

If you have more ticks than crosses you probably think that Richard was guilty. If you have more crosses than ticks you ought to give him the benefit of the doubt and find him not guilty.

Clue A

In 1674 the bones of two children were found in the Tower of London. They were in a wooden chest about 3 metres underground. People thought they were the bones of the princes. In 1933 scientists examined the bones but they could not prove whether the children were related or exactly how old they were. The bones do not give any clues about how the children died. They have not been examined since.

Clue B

There are no records of the princes being alive after the summer of 1483.

Clue C

Evidence from Dominic Mancini, an Italian priest. He was in London in 1483. He probably knew Edward V's doctor. Mancini left England in July 1483 and told his story many times to a bishop in France, who asked him to write the story down in the autumn of 1483.

Edward V's servants were prevented from seeing him. He and his brother were taken into the inner rooms of the Tower. Day by day they were seen less often behind the bars and windows until they were not seen at all. The King's doctor was the last servant to see him. He reported that the young king, like a victim ready to be sacrificed, believed that death was facing him. I have seen many men burst into tears when the young king was mentioned. Already people suspected that he had been murdered. How he has been murdered and whether he has been murdered at all I have not discovered.

Clue D

Richard's motto was 'Loyalty binds me'. He was very loyal to his brother, Edward IV, during a civil war in 1470. Richard was also a very religious man.

Clue E

In 1483 various men who had known and trusted Richard for years unexpectedly rebelled against him. Instead they decided to support Henry Tudor, a man they did not know at all.

Clue F

A year after the princes disappeared, their mother returned to Richard's court and allowed her daughter to dance with Richard.

Clue G

In the summer of 1483 Richard did order the executions of several men who tried to stop him becoming king. No trials were held before they were executed.

Clue H

Many northerners stayed loyal to Richard when others rebelled. When the leaders of the City of York heard that Richard had been killed they wrote in their records:

King Richard, who lawfully reigned over us, was defeated because of great treason by many men who turned against him. He was piteously murdered to the great heaviness [sadness] of this city.

(2) Have you any more ideas about who might have produced the interpretation of Richard on pages 18 and 19?

(3) Who do you think might have a more sympathetic interpretation of Richard?

■ **Why are there different interpretations of Richard?**

There are books, plays, films, websites and even a museum dedicated to Richard III. In some of them he is an evil murderer. In others he is a good, loyal man who was also a successful king.

(1) These cartoons explain why interpretations of Richard vary. What explanations can you work out from these scenes?

1

> I want people to hate Richard and be glad that I am now king. I will employ the best writers to make sure everyone believes that Richard murdered the princes.

2

> I need an exciting story to bring people to the theatre. The crowds always enjoy a really evil villain. I'll write a play about Richard III. People will love it ...

▲ ... and they did. Shakespeare's *Richard III* is still playing to packed theatres over 400 years later.

3

> I don't know for certain. There are no documents to prove that Richard killed the princes. But none that prove he didn't. Nobody knows for certain what happened to them.

> So do you think Richard III murdered his nephews?

4

> In some ways Richard was a good king. He was intelligent, he worked hard and he was a good soldier.

> That's true, but he was also violent and ruthless. He was a mix of very different qualities

The Big Ideas

History is . . .

full of interpretations. An interpretation is a version of history.

■ The first thing you do with an interpretation is **test** it against the evidence.

■ Then you **explain** it. That means understanding why someone made it and how that affects what they write or say.

You have been practising both skills in this zone.

. . . but watch out! Some interpretations are easier to spot than others!

The story of Richard III is an extreme example of someone, in this case Henry Tudor, wanting to interpret history a particular way for his or her own purposes. However, there are less obvious examples. In fact any writing about history – even a film or a museum display – is an interpretation, because someone somewhere has had to **select** what facts to include and decide **how to present** them.

Think

? Do you think a piece of History homework is an interpretation of history? <u>Why</u>?

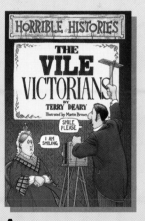

A

B

C

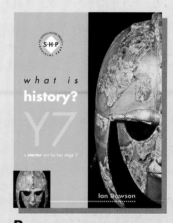

D

1 These pictures present some interpretations of history. You need to match each of them to one (or more) of these aims:

■ to entertain
■ to bring in visitors
■ to sell more copies
■ to provide accurate information
■ to make history as interesting as possible
■ to make you laugh.

2 Do you think the maker's aim might affect their interpretation? If so, how?

WHAT NEXT?
Which zone are you going to investigate next? Turn to pages 2–3 to see the choices.

zone ■ interpretation zone ■ interpretation zone ■ interpretation zone ■ interpretation zone ■ interpretation zone ■ interpretation

23

4 Why did they go to America?

Thousands of people emigrated from Britain to America in the 1600s. Nowadays that journey only takes a few hours by plane – but it wasn't so easy then. It took many weeks by ship and it was very dangerous. On one trip, 100 out of 450 people died of disease. One way or another, the travellers knew they had probably said goodbye to family and friends for ever . . .

1 Look at these illustrations and work out why people decided to risk such dangers to go to America. Make a list of the main reasons.

1 1649–1660

"England should be ruled by a king. I am not staying to be ruled by Parliament."

"I dare not stay in England now that there is a king again."

John Washington
In 1649 Parliament executed King Charles I and ruled the country without a king. Many of Charles' supporters (called Royalists) went to America. John Washington was among them.

William Goffe
signed the death warrant to execute Charles I. Eleven years later Charles' son became king and wanted the regicides (or 'king killers') put on trial. Goffe fled to America.

2 1741

"Goodbye England. I would rather have been whipped than sent to America."

Elizabeth Hardy
was deserted by her husband in London and left with no money. She stole goods worth less than a pound. She was only 19 but she was sentenced to transportation to America for life.
    In the 1700s 70 per cent of London's criminals suffered the same fate. Charles Scoldwell was even transported for life for stealing two ducks.

3 1760s

"We don't know what America is like but it cannot be worse than starving at home."

James MacMichael
had once been an army officer. He was one of the many Irish and Scots who travelled to America in the 1700s. He left Ireland because people paid high rents for their farmland but still faced death from starvation because, year after year, harvests were poor. If they tried to get work in the towns the wages were so low that they still could not buy enough food to eat. Despite his previous status, when James arrived in America he felt that he was 'looked upon as a barbarian'.

4 1762

> Captured, sold, then sold again! One day I will be free to choose where I live.

Olaudah Equiano

was a slave. He was captured in West Africa aged ten, and was sold to an owner in Britain. In 1762 he was sold to a slave owner in the West Indies.

But Equiano was one of the few slaves whose story had a happy ending. He scraped together enough money to buy his freedom and went on to campaign against slavery for the rest of his life.

After he gained his freedom Equiano took jobs on sea-going ships, and in 1773 he took part in a voyage of exploration to the North Pole; one of the other crew members was fifteen-year-old Horatio Nelson (see pages 28–31).

Equiano eventually returned to England and in 1789 wrote a book about his life which was a great success. He married an Englishwoman and had a family.

5 1606

> America! Is there anything more exciting than exploring a new country? I wonder what other adventures I'll have?

Captain John Smith

travelled to America with one of the first groups of English settlers. He was just 26 but had been travelling round Europe since he was 15, fighting as a soldier for most of the time. In America the settlers struggled to grow enough food so Smith volunteered to contact the local Indians. However, the Indians captured him and were about to execute him when the chief's daughter, Pocahontas, saved his life. After that the Indians helped the settlers until Smith returned to England.

6 1630–1641

> God is helping us to escape the King's religious laws. Soon we shall be able to pray as God wants us to.

Anne Bradstreet and John Winthrop

were Puritans. Between 1630 and 1641 80,000 Puritans travelled to America from Britain so that they could use their simple religious services. They hated the religious services that King Charles I was forcing on his people. Anne later became a poet. John was a lawyer who became a political leader in America.

Think

? Which helped you most in this task: the pictures, the descriptions or the word bubbles? <u>Why</u>?

Here is our list of REASONS why
people crossed the Atlantic.

Religion: to worship how they wanted.
Politics: because they were against the way
the country was governed.
A better life: to escape poverty.
Adventure: to explore exciting places and
perhaps make a fortune.

1 Do you agree with our list?

2 Which reason goes with each group
of people? (Be careful – we have
deliberately missed out one reason
from the list.)

1600

1606
Captain John Smith

1630–1641
Anne Bradstreet and
John Winthrop

1650

1649–1660
William Goffe and
John Washington

1700

1741
Elizabeth Hardy

1750

1762
Olaudah Equiano

1760s
James MacMichael

Think
? When people today
decide to leave one
country and move to
another do you think
they have <u>similar</u> or
<u>different</u> REASONS to the
people on this page?

1800

26

The Big Ideas

History is . . .

working out reasons why things happened. In the Why? Zone you started with a question – why did people leave Britain to go to America? And you should have found that there wasn't just one reason, or CAUSE, there were lots! So . . . when you have a 'Why?' question don't just look for one reason, or one result. There's usually more than one.

Different people had different reasons. But even that is too simple. In fact a *single* person or group might *combine* more than one reason.

1 Look at the picture below which shows a group of Puritans. Compare it with what the Puritan in picture 6 on page 25 had to say. What can you learn from this picture about explaining reasons in History?

> Life is so difficult because the harvests are so poor. We have to work so hard just to have enough to eat. Life will surely be a little easier in America.

> We will live a simple religious life in America. This will be a good example for other English people to copy.

> I want to get away from the King's religion. It is wrong.

> We must help the Indians to become Christians.

WHAT NEXT?
Which zone are you going to investigate next? Turn to pages 2–3 to see the choices.

zone ■ why? zone ■ why? zone ■ why? zone ■ why? zone ■ why? zone ■ why? zone ■ why? zone

27

Was Horatio Nelson really so significant?

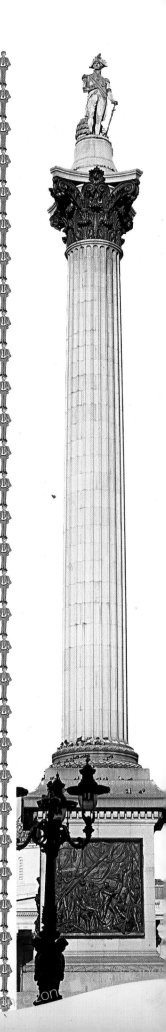

Horatio Nelson is one of the most famous names in British history. He was such a great hero that his statue was placed on top of the tallest column in the world (at that time), right in the centre of Britain's biggest city, London.

Nelson's Column is so high that you would need to stand more than thirty teachers on top of each other to reach the top. The statue of Nelson on the very top is at least another three teachers tall!

This is the kind of memorial people usually only get if they are really SIGNIFICANT. In this Significance Zone you will decide whether you think Nelson was really so significant.

1 As you read the story on the next two pages fill in a chart like this. You can get a sheet from your teacher to help you.

Reasons why Nelson was famous in his lifetime	Reasons why Nelson was significant in history

Think

? <u>What</u> is the difference between being famous and being significant?

? Can you <u>think</u> of someone who is famous but not significant?

1 'To be a hero'

Nelson always wanted to be a hero. He joined the navy in 1770 when he was twelve years old. Despite often being seasick, Nelson was promoted quickly and was captain of his own ship by the time he was 21.

In 1793 war broke out between Britain and France. Now Nelson had the chance he had always wanted – 'to be a hero'.

2 Wounded!

- In 1794 Nelson's right eye was badly damaged when he was hit by splinters from a cannon ball. After that he could only see light and dark with that eye. But he did not quit.
- In 1797 Nelson's right arm had to be amputated when a musket ball shattered the bones above the elbow. Still he did not quit. The sleeve tucked inside his jacket almost became his trademark.

3 *The hero of the Nile*

In 1798 the French army and navy sailed towards India, the richest part of Britain's empire. Nelson pursued them and cornered them near Egypt. At the Battle of the Nile he destroyed the French fleet, thereby ending the danger to India.

All over Britain, people rang church bells and lit bonfires to celebrate. Every house seemed to have a picture of Nelson in the window!

4 The Nelson Touch

Nelson was not just a hero at home. His sailors liked and respected him because he was brave but he treated his men fairly and well. He was especially kind to the young sailors who were fighting in a battle for the first time.

5 Napoleon is coming: who can stop him?

This is the Emperor Napoleon of France, one of the greatest generals in history. By 1805 Napoleon controlled most of Europe. His next target was Britain.

6 Invasion alert

Napoleon planned an invasion. He gathered an army of 100,000 soldiers on the French coast. It was such a large army that its white tents, reflecting the sunlight, could be seen across the English Channel. Napoleon built a fleet of barges to sail his soldiers to England. Now all he needed was for his ships to arrive from Spain to protect the barges.

In Britain, people built beacons on the coast. As soon as the French landed the beacons would be lit and the news would reach London in just two minutes. Weapons were given out for defence.

But Nelson had other ideas about how to protect England . . . He did not wait for Napoleon's ships to come to him: he went to them – all the way to Cadiz (in the south of Spain).

1 On the rest of this page we have not written headlines for each block. We have left that up to you. Write them on another sheet.

7 ?

On 21 October 1805 the two navies faced each other at Cape Trafalgar.

Nelson sent orders to all his ships: 'England expects that every man will do his duty.'

Gunners spread sawdust on the decks to stop themselves slipping in the blood that would soon be spilt. Sailors stripped to the waist to save the surgeons having to cut away their shirts if they were wounded.

Nelson dressed in his admiral's uniform. His medals gleamed on his chest.

8

Then Nelson took the French completely by surprise. Instead of sailing his ships parallel to the French ships and firing guns at them, Nelson drove his ships straight at the French line. This was a completely new tactic and it won the battle.

The French scattered in chaos. The British ships chased them. Eighteen French ships were sunk or captured.

9

Britain was safe from invasion . . . but Nelson was dead. In the thick of battle a French soldier fired down from the rigging of his ship, fatally wounding Nelson.

As Nelson died, his last words were 'Thank God I have done my duty.' One sailor said that when the news spread, 'Chaps that fought like the devil sat down and cried like a wench [a woman].'

10

Nelson's body was brought back to London. Thousands lined the streets for his funeral. They bought cups and plates, badges and even ladies' clothing with his picture on. The poet Robert Southey said 'England has had many heroes but never a hero who was so completely loved by his fellow countrymen.'

11 ?

For the next hundred years, Britain's navy was the most powerful in the world. It helped make Britain rich because the navy protected its trading ships. No other country dared to challenge Britain.

Significance Zone

The Big Ideas

History is...

deciding who or what is significant ... and why. To be significant in history is more than being famous.

In 2002 the BBC ran a poll called 'Great Britons'. People voted for the person they thought was the greatest Briton in history. This caused a lot of argument. Some of the people in the top 100 were very famous or popular (like singers or footballers) – but were they really significant? Nelson came in the top ten in the Great Britons poll! Do you think he was really that significant? Here is a list of CRITERIA that make some people significant in history.

Reasons for being significant	Horatio Nelson
1) If he or she changed events at the time they lived	
2) If he or she improved lots of people's lives – or made them worse!	
3) If he or she changed people's ideas	
4) If he or she had a long-lasting impact on their country or the world	
5) If he or she had been a really good or a very bad example to other people of how to live or behave	

1 On your own copy of the chart above, give Nelson a mark out of 4 for each criterion. Use your completed chart from page 28 to help you.

2 **a)** Which aspect of history (right) interests you most? Why?
   b) Which aspect do you think is most significant? Why?
   c) Can you think of anyone in history who was more significant than Nelson?
   d) Was Nelson so significant that everyone should study him in school?

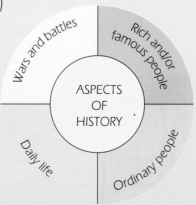

Wars and battles
Rich and/or famous people
ASPECTS OF HISTORY
Daily life
Ordinary people

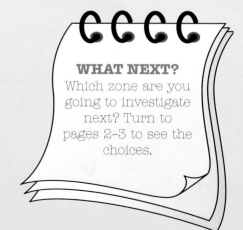

WHAT NEXT?
Which zone are you going to investigate next? Turn to pages 2–3 to see the choices.

6 What was it like to arrive in Britain?

Empathy Zone

In June 1948, 500 West Indians arrived in Britain on board the SS *Empire Windrush*.

It was three years after the end of the Second World War. Britain was short of workers – particularly drivers, nurses and factory workers, but other kinds of workers as well. They advertised in the West Indies (the Caribbean). Over the next ten years, 125,000 West Indians came to Britain. What was it like for these people to arrive and live in a new country?

We call working out what people in the past thought and felt 'EMPATHY'. That is what the Empathy Zone is all about. You will be using extracts from interviews with people who came to Britain in the 1940s and 1950s to help you find out what they thought and how they felt.

1. Before you start examining the sources, think about how people might feel. Jot down a few words that best describe what it might have felt like to have arrived in Britain from the West Indies on the *Empire Windrush* in 1948.

2. Work with a partner. Study Sources A–I in turn (or as many as you have time for). Make a list of the words or phrases that describe what it felt like to be a West Indian immigrant. Use the words in the sources or other words that describe those feelings.

EMPIRE WINDRUSH
LONDON

empathy zone empathy zone empathy zone emp

► Source A Immigrants from Jamaica arriving at Newhaven, 22 September 1958.

▼ Source B Many West Indians came to Britain to fight in the Second World War. Some, like these men, were pilots in the RAF. Of the 250 men who came from Trinidad, 52 were killed. Euton Christian was one West Indian who came to Britain to join the RAF in 1944. He returned to Jamaica in 1947 and then came back to Britain on the *Empire Windrush*. He became a town councillor in Manchester. He remembered:

When we first came over we were more or less welcomed because we were in uniform. But when the war ended, they were saying to themselves, 'Well, okay lads, you've been over here now for two or three year, you won the war for us, go back home now, isn't it about time you go back home?' That was the message. It wasn't spelt out but that's what it was.

▼ **Source C** Cecil Holness joined the RAF in 1944. He returned to Jamaica in 1947 and then came back to Britain on the *Empire Windrush*. He lived in London and worked as a motor mechanic.

Just when we got married, 1949, and I saw this advert in a shop window about rooms to let and then when I phoned the lady, she say, 'Oh yes, come round, it's all here, you'll get the room.' So when I arrive, I rang the bell and this white lady she came out and I said 'Good afternoon madam', and the moment when she answered the door you know it's like as if she's so frightened because she didn't expect to see a black man. She said 'No, I haven't got any room to let. I don't want black people.'

▼ **Source D** From an interview with Londoners who came to Britain in the 1950s, published in *Reform*, a church magazine, in 1998.

Berris Anderson: 'I worked for seven weeks at British Rail and then the foreman got rid of us. This white chap was working there and he had a fire and when we went there to try to warm our hands he moved away and went to get the foreman. He called us to the office and said "On Friday, you finish". All seven of us. We were treated different but that was the only place while I've been here.'

Pearline Wynter: 'Well, the welcome was very good for me, I didn't find any fault with it. And up to now in this country I have never had trouble with anyone. I can't give anyone a bad name for that.'

▼ **Source E** Connie Mark came to Britain in 1954 to join her husband who was a professional cricketer playing for clubs in the north-east. She worked in the NHS until she retired.

When I came, I saw everybody going into their little houses, and then nobody spoke to you. That never happened in Jamaica. As long as you met somebody in the street, it's good morning, good evening and hello. And [here] you find you're saying to somebody good morning and they never answered you, and then you felt stupid after that, so you stopped saying good morning.

▼ **Source F** Ivan Weekes came to Britain in 1955. He later became a local councillor in Chelsea. Here he is describing attitudes at the time of the race riots in 1958.

I used to feel not only frightened but wondering what's going to happen next. I could get bumped off. You would get on a bus and the atmosphere on the bus was electric. You could cut the air with a knife, the tension. People would talk in whispers: 'You hear what happened last night? You hear who got shot?' And people would look at you, like spears, daggers. People would spit at you. Nobody spit at me personally but I know that happened. If you went to sit down beside somebody on a bus they'd shuffle up. But then somebody would look at you, see that you're frightened as hell and say, 'Oh mate, take no notice of them, we're not all the same.' I think that's so important to say. That was my experience, 'take no notice of them, we're not all the same.' And just those few words gave me two things: hope and comfort. People were not all the same.

▼ **Source G** Vince Reid came to Britain on the *Empire Windrush*, aged 13. He left school without any qualifications. He joined the RAF but later studied at Sussex University, trained as a teacher and taught in London until he retired.

When I went to school, first of all, I was a subject of curiosity, which is quite surprising when you think that you had black soldiers in England. And people would come up and rub your skin and see if it would rub off the black, and rub your hair, and, you know, it's really insulting. And of course there was always the latent violence, people wanting to fight you.

I was the only black child in the school. They didn't even give me a test to see which grade I should be put in, they just put me in the lowest grade. Then they had a sort of end of year examination and I moved up into the top class. But I remember a teacher teaching Shakespeare and he said 'Who can explain what this soliloquy means?' So I put my hand up. Of course the way I spoke then is not like I speak now, I had this funny Jamaican accent. And this teacher just rolled around. I felt so ashamed, that he was basically mocking me. And I really stopped going to school because I felt so angry and ashamed. It still hurts to this day. You weren't expected to know anything and they just took the mickey. That was 1949 and it still hurts.

▼ **Source H** Aldwyn Roberts was a calypso singer known as Lord Kitchener. He was one of the passengers on board the *Empire Windrush*.

A friend told me I can get a job in The Sunset Club. I started singing this song. Of course, the Caribbean people understood the song and they explained it to their white friends. So, most of the people understood the song and then it became so popular I was singing in three clubs in one night. This went on for quite a while.

After this I had no worries. I was living like a king.

▼ **Source I** Tryphena Anderson arrived in Liverpool from Jamaica in 1952. She trained as a nurse in Nottingham.

I came from such a bright place, so much sunshine, so much colour, it was very depressing. I wished I could be back home so bad it hurts, because you missed the sort of freedom and companionship you used to have, you know, with your own kind. One day I was on a bus and I saw a black man. I just felt, if only this bus would stop, I would get off it and just run and hug him and find out, you know, where he came from.

1 As a class, now compile a complete list of words and phrases that describe what it felt like to be a West Indian immigrant in 1948.

2 Compare the class list with your words from task 1. Are they different? And if they are, why?

The Big Ideas

History is . . .

empathy – using sources to work out people's feelings and experiences. You will use empathy a lot in History, but you do NOT just *imagine* what life was like for people. In History you use sources to find out their feelings and experiences.

It's harder to find out the feelings of some people than of others – because we don't have enough sources to tell us what they were thinking.

1. What kinds of sources have been used in this zone to find out about the experiences of the people on the *Empire Windrush*?

2. Here are five people. Whose feelings do you think it would be easy to find out about and whose would be difficult?

Harald Hardrada – King of Norway 1045–1066

William Gladstone, Prime Minister when Queen Victoria was queen.

Robert Blincoe, a young factory worker who lived around 1800

Thomas Woodcock, a brewer who lived in Wymondham, Norfolk, when Elizabeth I was queen

Queen Elizabeth I

3. Are people's memories, such as those you've read in Sources A–I, likely to be <u>trustworthy</u> evidence?

. . . remember, there is always more than one answer to 'What was it like to . . .'

Different people have different experiences. You have already worked this out for yourselves from the sources in this zone. Whenever you study an event in history, you need to remember that people have different experiences, attitudes and reactions.

HAVE YOU NOTICED?

In every zone of this book you have met people.
History is ... about people – what they did, why they did it, how their lives were affected by events. In History it's people all the way!

4 Can you find the missing faces? Who are these people and which period did they live in? You have met all of them in this book.

1000 BC

500 BC

50 BC

AD 600

1066

1483

1762

1800

1948

AD 2000

WHAT NEXT?
Which zone are you going to investigate next? Turn to pages 2–3 to see the choices.

7 What does it mean to get better at History?

Improvement Zone

Congratulations! You have completed all our What is History? zones. The Improvement Zone is here to bring together some of the threads.

1 The illustrations below give some reminders of the enquiries you have followed. Can you match up these enquiries to the right zones?

Evidence Zone

INTERPRETATION ZONE

Why? Zone

Significance Zone

Empathy Zone

A

B

C

I deserve to be remembered for hundreds of years.

What about all the ordinary people who fought on your ship?

Don't they deserve to be remembered as well?

D

I'm leaving because I hate this king.

I'm leaving so I can make my fortune.

I've got no choice about leaving.

E

King Richard is a good man. We like him here in York.

This king is evil. He even had his nephews murdered so he could be king.

History is . . .

debate. You have probably spotted that in each enquiry there were debates and disagreements. History is full of these.

(2) Can you match up these debates to the right zones?

1

> The main reason why people went to America was religion. They didn't like the King's religious rules.

> That was important to some people but I think most went to get better housing and more food and money.

2

> You can't be completely certain. There isn't enough evidence to be definite.

> I'm certain those skeletons are the remains of the Vikings killed at the Battle of Stamford Bridge.

3

> My father told me he was given a good welcome in Britain. He found work quickly and he played cricket every weekend.

> He was one of the lucky ones. It wasn't like that for my family. They had to keep moving house because of racism. It took a few years to settle down.

4

> Richard III was a good man. All those northerners fought for him. They didn't believe he was a murderer.

> But what about the princes? They disappeared and were never seen again.

5

> Nelson was a really important man. He saved Britain from invasion.

> Important? The really important people were those who worked hard to improve the housing and working conditions of ordinary people. That's far more important to more people.

Think

? <u>Why</u> do you think there are lots of disagreements and debates in History? How many reasons can you think of?

? Do <u>you</u> think debates and disagreements make History more fun or more difficult? Your own opinion is important.

History is . . .

understanding the past. Through this book you have used different skills at different times. It helps you learn to do that. But History isn't just about using sources; or just explaining 'why' or any of the zones on their own. Our aim in History is to understand the past and to do that you need *all* the zones to work together.

Here is an example of how to use the zones together. This picture shows the execution of King Charles I in 1649. It was painted soon after the execution by a French artist. If you wanted to understand the people and events of the 1640s, you would need to ask questions about the picture from all the zones (and probably others as well that we have not covered).

① Work in pairs. Think of at least two questions from each of our zones that would help you understand this picture and the event it shows. Look back to pages 38–39 and the Big Ideas pages to help you. Usually you get marks for good answers; this time you get the best marks for the best questions!

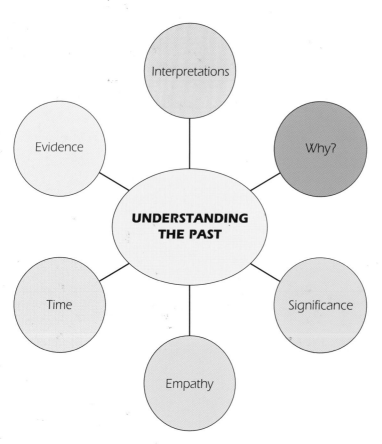

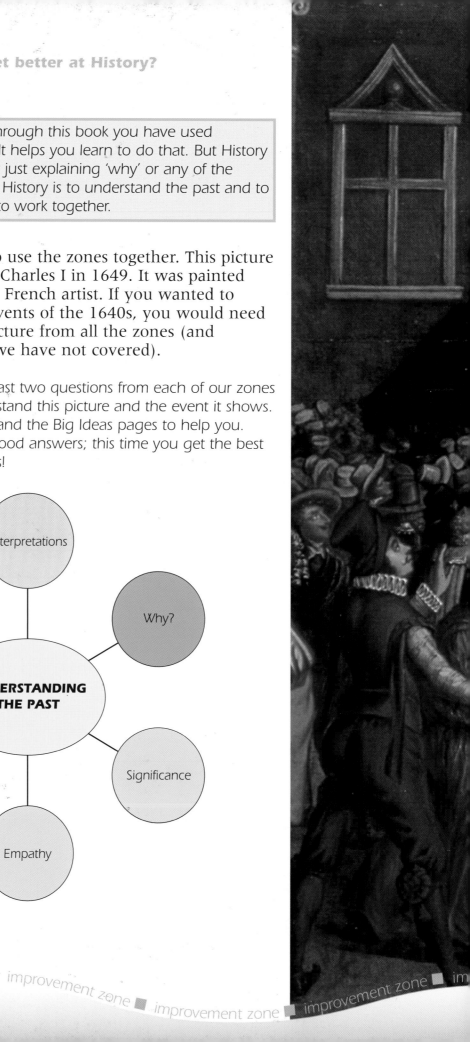

■ Getting better at History

Here's a quick activity that will show you how much you have learned about doing History.

1. Which of these pupils has got the best idea about how to get better at History? Can you think of another way of getting better at History to put on the tabard of pupil 9?

2. Rearrange the pupils so that the best ways of improving at History are closest to the Finishing Line.

!!!THE FINISHING LINE!!!
Getting Better at History Means...

1 Use coloured pens to underline your headings

2 Be able to decide how definite your answer is

3 Write longer answers

4 Know more dates and facts

5 Think out your own ideas and opinions using evidence

6 Remember that there are usually several reasons why something happens, not just one

Words! Words! Words!

And you'll get even better at History if you use the right vocabulary!

3 Can you explain what each of these words means?

chronology   artefact

medieval   reason

ancient   cause

modern   document

period   investigation

interpretation   enquiry

significance

hypothesis

empathy

archaeology

source

anachronism

evidence

criteria

The Getting Better at History Race

Understand how to use sources as evidence

Write very neatly

■ Using the Big Ideas

So now you know what History is all about. In that case it's time to move on and do some more! This board game shows you some of the people and events you may investigate over the next three years.

To play the game:

- Play in teams of two. It's your team against the rest of the class.
- Blue squares – stop at every blue square. On each blue square there is a question. You have to decide which of our zones the question belongs to. Make a list of your answers. You'll get two points for every right answer.
- Yellow squares – stop at every yellow square. Jot down one question about the topic on the square for the zone shown in the cloud. You'll score two points for each good question.
- Picture squares – you don't have to stop on these squares.
- At the end your teacher will give you the answers. Add up the points and see which team has won.

The Interpretation Zone

1455–1487

The Wars of the Roses

How do we know about life in the Middle Ages?

The Evidence Zone

1415

Henry V and the Battle of Agincourt

1348

Was the Black Death really so important?

1337–1453

100

The Hundred Years' War

The Empathy Zone

1066

START

Why did the Normans win the Battle of Hastings?

1095–1291

The Crusades

The Significance Zone

The Why? Zone

1170

Henry II and the murder of Thomas Becket

1215

Does everybody agree that King John was a terrible king?

What was it like to live in a castle in the Middle Ages?

1450s

Why was printing such an important invention?

1536

Why did Henry VIII shut down all the monasteries?

1558

How do we know about Queen Elizabeth I?

1588

The Spanish Armada

1605

The Gunpowder Plot

1642–1649

What was it like to fight in the Civil War?

1653

Why did Oliver Cromwell turn down the chance to be king?

The Evidence Zone

The Interpretation Zone

The Why? Zone

The Evidence Zone

1851

The Great Exhibition

1829

Stephenson's Rocket – the first railway

1800s

Did the British Empire improve people's lives in India?

1815

The Battle of Waterloo

1790s

The French Revolution

1666

The Great Fire of London

The Empathy Zone

1750–1900

What kinds of sources tell us about life during the Industrial Revolution?

The Significance Zone

The Significance Zone

The Interpretation Zone

FINISH

The Significance Zone

1913

Were the Suffragettes heroines?

1914

Assassination at Sarajevo

1914–1918

What was it like to be a soldier in the trenches?

1939

Why did World War II begin?

1940

The Battle of Britain

The Empathy Zone

1939–1945

Why was the Holocaust so important?

1945

First nuclear weapons

45

Index